The Night Library
Anna Robinson

with artwork by **Martin Parker**

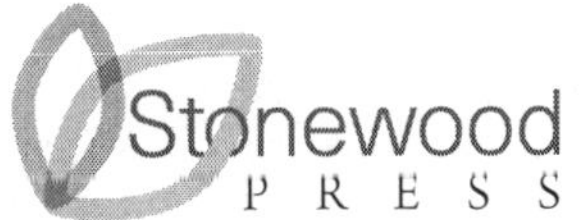

Stonewood PRESS

First published in 2015
by Stonewood Press
97 Benefield Road, Oundle PE8 4EU
Tel: 0845 456 4838 | books@stonewoodpress.co.uk
www.stonewoodpress.co.uk

ISBN: 978-1-910413-08-1

Distributed by Central Books, 99 Wallis Road, London E9 5LN
Email: orders@centralbooks.com | Tel: 0845 458 9911

Printed and bound in the UK by Imprintdigital, Exeter
Designed and typeset in Sabon 10.5pt/Palatino Light 13pt
by www.silbercow.co.uk

ACKNOWLEDGMENTS
The poems have been previously published in *Long Poem Magazine* and I owe
gratitude to a number of books, starting with Alberto Manguel's *The Library at
Night*. Books and articles about librarianship by James Duff Brown, Melvil Dewey,
Alfred Cotgreave, Charles A. Cutter, and Richard J Fritz, have also been used in the
production of these poems. Several real librarians are featured within, but I won't
embarrass them by specific mentions. *To all my librarians everywhere.* – AR

I would like to thank Jacqueline Gabbitas, Frances Barry and Mimi Khalvati for their
support, guidance and kind words about the artworks in this book. And Anna for
bringing the idea to me and Stonewood. – MP

"*The Night Library* is exactly what its name
implies: mysterious yet ordered, interrogated yet
known by touch, its makers embedded in not
just the texts but the furniture and very cosmos
they have created. If dreams have their sytems
so do libraries as Borges well knew. But this has
lyrical verse: spare yet full. Its commentaries are
under the skin." – George Szirtes

The Night Library

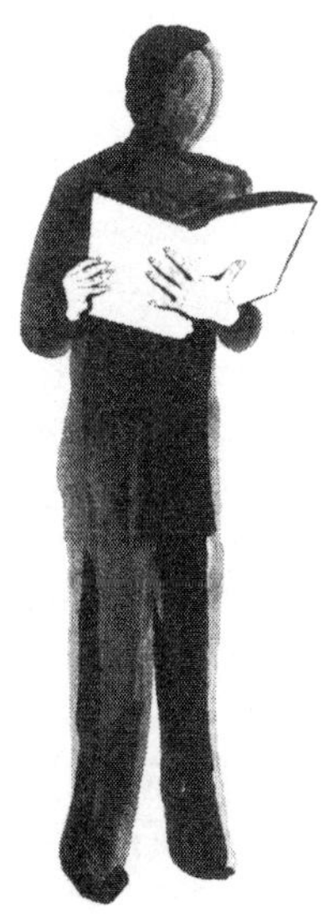

At night, left to their own devices, words rise
from their pages, using just their own warmth
to lift and hang and seek each other, like for like.

Sensing their sameness and shade, they drift,
starry, to group and regroup – cluster and clump –
outline their thoughts with a nod to old wisdom.

They swarm and buzz – spin heat and light
till the noise would wake you, if you were there.
And then, when they're ready, the indexes combine.

The departments of human knowledge are so

numerous –
dozens – dozens of rational systems to choose from –
each capable – the intersections so great –

there is not the slightest difficulty in working it out –
it does not matter as long as they are together,
one source, one germ, one fixed place.

Subjects overlap. Subjects qualify each other.
Subjects are capable and each of these may be
the centre of an enormous literature and an important study.[i]

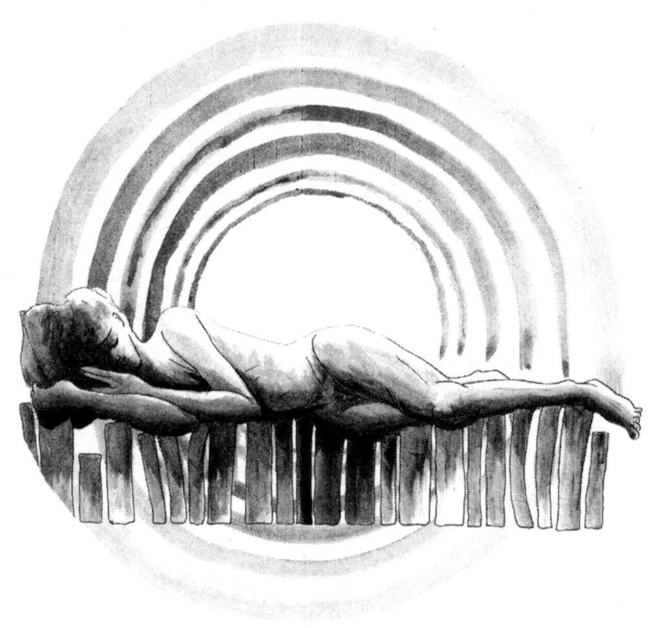

In the beautiful library, the beautiful librarian
stretches his long legs as he rises from his desk.
The desk is a dark oak whose age is shown
by rings and the marks of three hundred years
of writing with a fine pencil on hand-made paper.

He moves his body to the open shuttered
window that overlooks the square.
We are somewhere in Italy. This is unclassified.
The square is empty. The people have all gone home.
The stars of the Bear hang in the night sky.

His books are bound in cream, the shelves solid
like his desk – and each has its subject marked
in italic, hand-painted on an oval
plaque above. The beautiful librarian is tired.

He closes the windows and shutters and goes to his bed
in the alcove. As he sleeps, the books open.
It's now I learn that his name is Francisco.

Anonymous books are to be entered

*under the
name of the author whenever it is known.*[ii]
Question the publisher, and if they refuse to tell
you, follow them and see who they meet and who
they drink with. Failing that – display the book
and see who comes and stands and stares longest
at the title or see who does not come and who
does not look at all. Failing that – see what you
learn when you sleep.

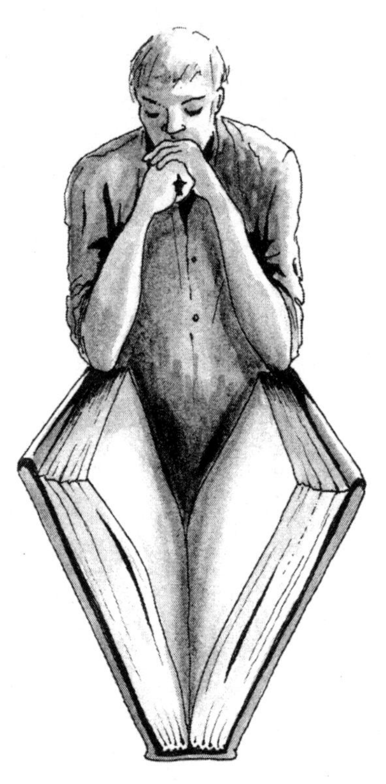

In the burning library the books are fierce and dry.
Their pages are as brittle as the dead wood they grew from
and bent as coughing hags. Depending on the subject matter
the flames dance lightly on the leaves or writhe across drafts
or thrash about in doorways. If they find the space,
they rush it, explode to fit, filling it with bright orange light.

The rules of the burning library are as follows: no water,
only pencils in the reading room, you must bring with you
everything you need to survive, you may not do anything,
you may not do nothing. The burning librarian
is large and rigid. All is sacrificed, herself included.

No reduction is permissible.

All the letters –
          all the words they form,
          their punctuation, the spaces
     between and around –
all matter and all must be –
there is no repetition –
     this A is not this A –
          it is itself only – whatever
          it may remind you of.
     The code is an imposter.
The labyrinth a trap.

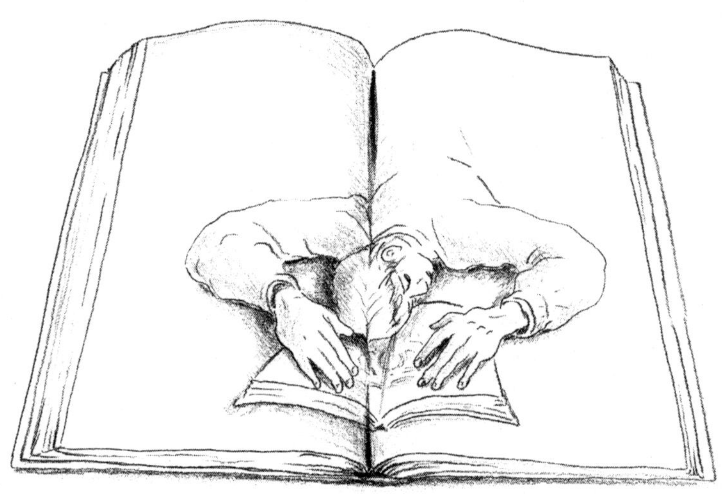

In our dreams, the library has no limits.
The chief librarian ponders this on a warm night
waking, once again, from a slippery sleep.
Every night, when he closes his eyes, somewhere
in the world, more books are being written.
His library is full, and yet also incomplete.
The chief librarian lies on his bed in his underpants.
More space might be the solution, more shelving.
The chief librarian considers what can be added,
he flutters his third eye on every shelf
he could build, in every house, the town hall,
in the shops and cafés, and when every indoor wall
has shelves, he will start on the outer ones –
extending the roofs to provide cover – adding
glass doors to protect them from driving rain.
And when every outdoor wall has shelves – the walls
of the city itself will be shelved and when they are full
he will tunnel, build book caves in a downward spiral.
The chief librarian smiles and strokes his round belly.
His books will be housed, no matter how many.

The fixed field has no sub-fields.

The fixed field is so called because it always contains forty bytes of data. It is non-repeatable. If a record type is coded *a* then 19 elements are defined. If a record type is coded *m* then 15 elements are defined. No matter what – 8 elements are always present – these are the things people will want to know. If a code for an element is longer than one character, its starting and ending positions are indicated.[iii]

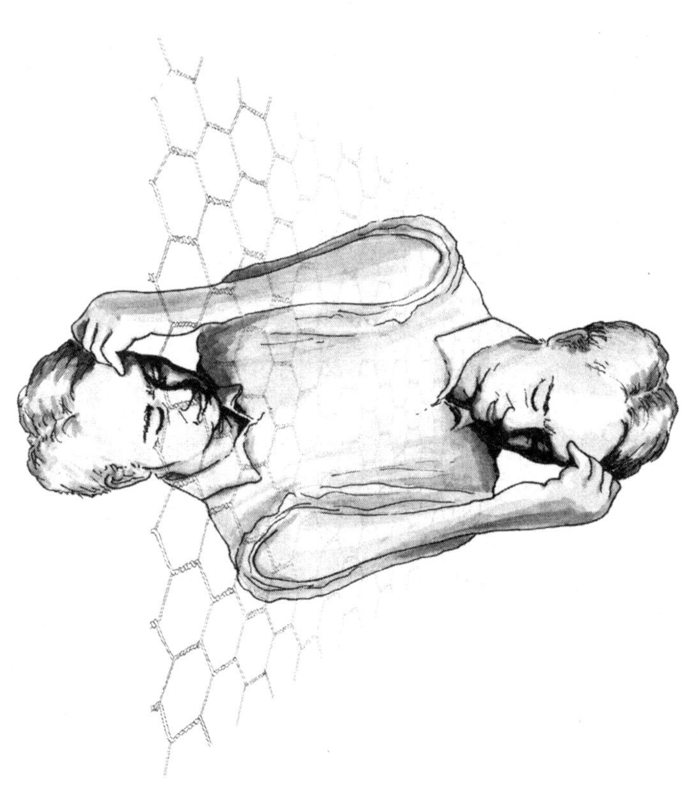

The banned books look disorderly, unstricted,
organised purely by author – they nestle, comfortable,
on their solid shelves behind the chicken wire.
These are big narratives and will wipe doubt away.
In daylight, the way they stand, you'd think them silent
but at midnight, when the words fly, they battle:
science, ideology, gods; sparking little fires
only they can put out. Although he never sees this,
the librarian knows and worries, though he thinks
he has the stock balance right for now! His hair
is grey and hard to keep neat and sleep is not always easy.

I dreamed night and day that there must be

*somewhere a
satisfactory solution.* All my ideas were floating,
everything I know and do and am and every word
I have ever read or heard or spoken and every book
and every tree and every star and I knew from
early, in one dream, that the solution was number
and then one day in church, during a long sermon,
the answer *flasht over me, decimals, and like this I
could classify all human knowledge in print.*[iv]

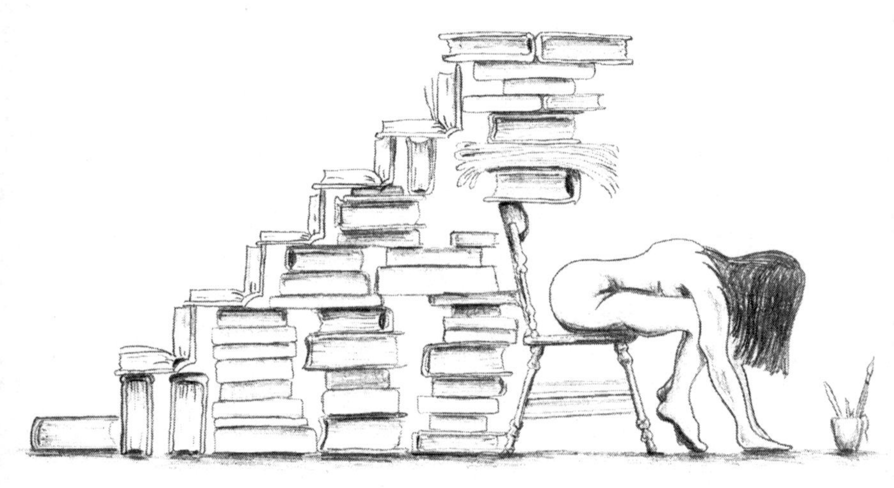

In the well-ordered library, the well-ordered librarian
is mixing stain removers. She measures equal amounts
of calamine, salt and alum and sets them to boil
in white wine. The brush she will use is fine.
The sheets of white blotting paper lie in wait.
This is how she removes ink stains; for grease
she has set out ether and benzoline and is warming
an iron. She has a book to tell her what to do.
It says *when the stain is caused by a slice
of bacon having been used as a book-mark,
or by contact with a paraffin lamp, the borrower
should be asked to remove it and supply a new copy.*[v]
It is late and she should have gone home.

You will discover the layout of the library

                                   and what books
are placed where. The book you need to find
          is not listed, so you need

to work out, by yourself, that it is located in T.1.1.
    Straight ahead from where you enter is section A.
          To the right of section A and furthest

from the entrance is section B. Look for the book.
    You don't have much time from when you enter. You can
        only summon help when you have entered.

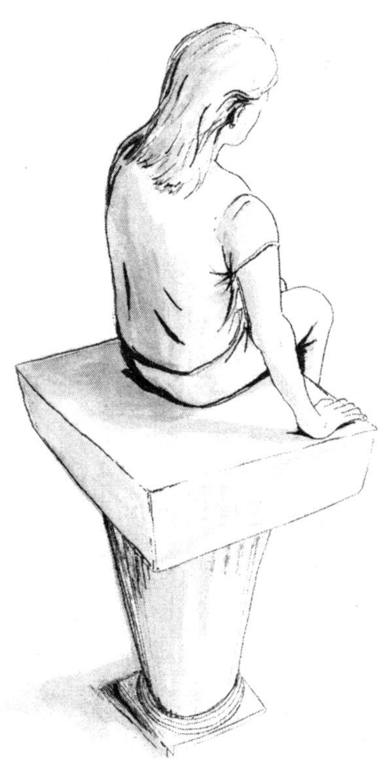

In the stone library great store is placed on sand.
Aside from that it is pretty much as you'd expect
with its tablets and casements, et cetera.
There are columns in the central hall, each
with capitals; and the stones in the walls, upper
and lower case. This librarian is both a mason
and printer and her hands are large. She chisels
her catalogue and typesets the shelving.

The rare books section is protected by ivy
and little birds flit in and out. They are the indexers
and can sing you any précis you like.

In the golden section there are headless statues.
There is dust on the floor and it maps the shape
of the space where you read.

The shelves can be raised or lowered

*by one
person without removing or disarranging the
books… No space is lost: no mechanism to get
jammed… or nip the fingers: no dangers to
bindings by projecting metal… no tilting of
shelves. These are testimonials: As the library has
been open nearly twelve months, I can speak with
confidence on this matter. Having had experience
of every kind of shelf fittings now in general use,
both in England and America, I can firmly
recommend this system.*[vi]

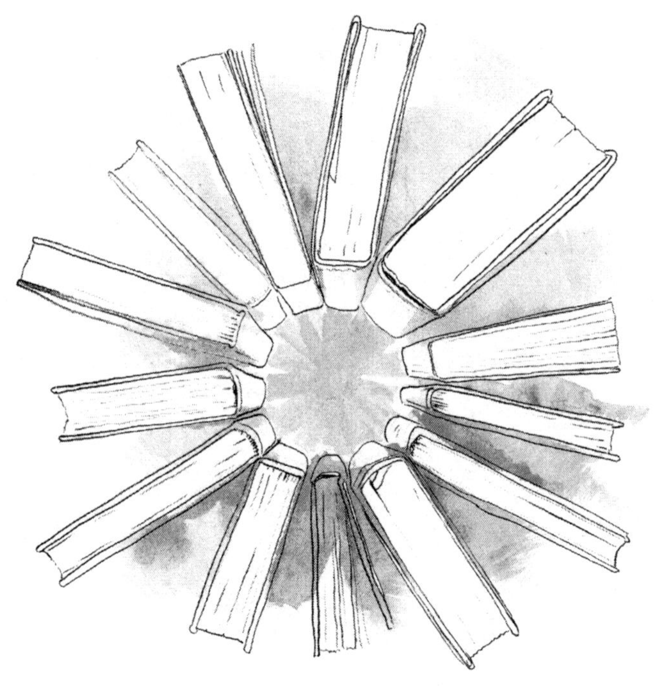

The shape of the library is always round, even
when it's not. The books think this for you;
arcing towards each other for all their walled lives.

They arc off rolling stacks forming circles.
Within and between the pages the words press
to make polka dots and all the stories join up.

Their ends and beginnings merge to form
a single note. Any decent librarian will try
to tame them as sometimes they won't bend back.

The heat of the library must be temperate,
you must not cram too many in one place. The tendency
of books to arc can only ever be managed.

Librarians were born

in Tongue, in Lever Bridge, in the Old Buildings of the British Library, in Blackburn, Hackney, Seighford, Felling, Cardiff, Leeds and Leek. There are many other places too that can birth a librarian and these are too numerous to mention.[vii]

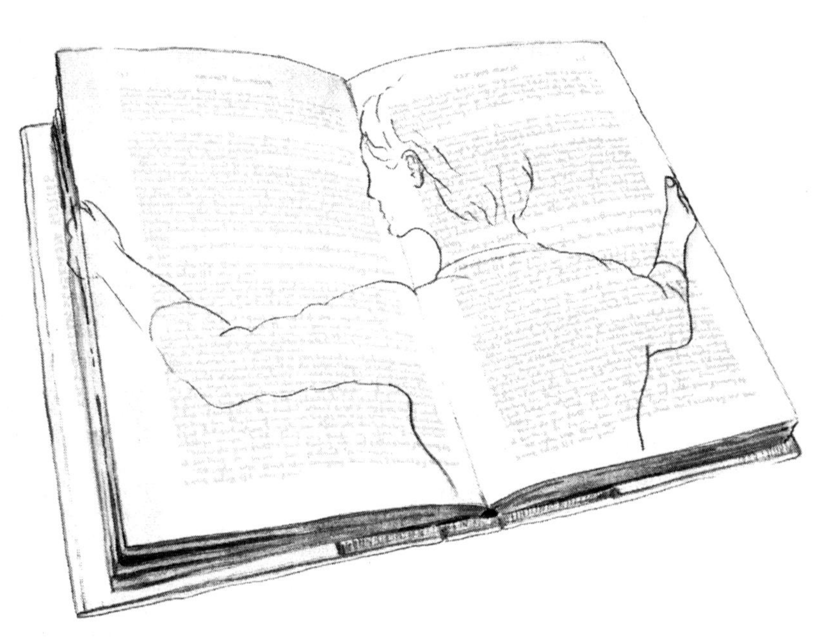

When the librarian dies, the books will mourn.
For them, there's no one who knows them like her
no matter how devoted their readers have been.

She knows their weight and smell and who sits best
with whom and if not how, she at least knows
when each got its scars; she has patched them,

kept them clean and made a note
of their whole lives. She's not their mother!
She can be replaced. But they will hold

the spit of her, in their pages and fabric
for as long as they survive.

Notes

i   James Duff Brown, 1897, *Classification and Cataloguing, The Library*, Vol 9: p. 149 and James Duff Brown, 1914, *Subject Classification with tables, indexes etc., for the sub-division of subjects*, 2nd ed., London: Grafton

ii   Charles A Cutter, 1904, *Rules for a dictionary catalog*, Fourth edition, Government Printing Office, Washington, USA

iii   Richard J Fritz, 2003, Marc21 for Everyone, ALA Editions

iv   Melvil Dewey, *Decimal Classification Beginning, in Library Journal 45 2/15/20*

v   James Duff Brown, 1909, *Guide to Librarianship*, London: Libraco

vi   Advert for Simplex Shelving Systems, in Alfred Cotgreave, 1901, *Views and Memoranda of Public Libraries*, London: Library Aids Co.

vii Biographical detail from Alfred Cotgreave, 1901, *Views and Memoranda of Public Libraries*, London: Library Aids Co.

The artwork throughout *The Night Library* is made using pencil, pen, water colour and inks.

ANNA ROBINSON was born and lives in London. Her first collection *The Finders of London* (Enitharmon Press) was shortlisted for the Seamus Heaney Poetry Centre Prize (2011). *Into The Woods* was published in 2014 (Enitharmon Press). She has taught at the University of East London, The Poetry School, HMP Brixton, as well as in schools, libraries and public record offices. Anna has also been (and no doubt will be again one day) a librarian. She is currently the chair of the Friends of Waterloo Library. www.annarobinsonpoetry.co.uk

MARTIN PARKER has a BA in Photography from Napier University, Edinburgh and an MA in Fine Art from Central Saint Martin's, London. He has worked as a freelance graphic designer since 2000, focusing his work in the arts and education sectors. His art has been exhibited in Edinburgh, Sheffield, London and abroad and his artwork has also featured on several books, magazines and album covers.

Other Stonewood Press titles:

Dad's slideshow by Di Slaney

Hoad and other stories by Sarah Passingham

Small Grass poems by Jacqueline Gabbitas with artwork by Frances Barry

Earthworks by Jacqueline Gabbitas

Notebook in hand: New and Selected Poems by John Rety

Said and done: New Writing from Brittle Star edited Louisa Hooper, Jacqueline Gabbitas, David Floyd and Martin Parker, with a foreword by Maureen Duffy

www.stonewoodpress.co.uk